Drivers'
Handbook

Richard Porter

DISCLAIMER

Every effort has been made to ensure that the
information presented in this handbook is correct,
especially after last year. However, whilst the
Top Gear Motoringists' Association regrets the
offence caused by much of the content of last year's
edition, we can accept no responsibility for any
errors, omissions or for the inclusion of a graphic
story about a well-known actor and a glass coffee
table which later turned out to be untrue.

This book is published to accompany the television series entitled Top Gear.
Executive Producer: Andy Wilman

1 3 5 7 9 10 8 6 4 2

Published in 2011 by BBC Books, an imprint of Ebury Publishing.
A Random House Group Company

Picture credits: all photographs Shutterstock except: p.61 t © Jeff Morgan 16/Alamy; p.61 b © Danita Delimont/Alamy; p.62 © Getty Images; p.63 © The Marsden Archive/Alamy; p.65 © 42pix/Alamy; p. 67 t © mediablitzimages (uk) Limited/Alamy; p.67 b © Gwendolyn Plath/Getty Images; p. 68 © Imagestate Media Partners Limited - Impact Photos/Alamy; p.72 © Norma Brazendale/Alamy; p. 73 courtesy of Boots the Chemist; p. 74 t © Colin Underhill/Alamy; p.75 © The National Trust Photolibrary/Alamy; p. 76 © Tim Jones/Alamy; p.115 © jo stephens/Alamy; p.117 t © Mike Abrahams/Alamy; p.117 b © Mode Images Limited/Alamy; p. 118 b © SNAP/Rex Features; p.119 © Robert Bird/Alamy; p. 120 © Emmanuel LATTES/Alamy.

The Random House Group Limited Reg. No. 954009

Addresses for companies within the Random House Group can be found at
www.randomhouse.co.uk

A CIP catalogue record for this book is available from the British Library.

ISBN 978 1 84 990153 6

The Random House Group Limited supports the Forest Stewardship Council (FSC), the leading international forest certification organisation. All our titles that are printed on Greenpeace approved FSC certified paper carry the FSC logo. Our paper procurement policy can be found at www.randomhouse.co.uk/environment

Commissioning editor: Lorna Russell
Editor: Caroline McArthur
Copy-editor: Ian Gittins
Designer: Jim Lockwood
Illustrations: The Comic Stripper

Printed and bound in Germany by GGP Media GmbH, Pössneck

To buy books by your favourite authors and register for offers, visit www.randomhouse.co.uk

PRINCIPAL CONTENTS

Contrary to earlier information, this contents listing applies only to
Top Gear Drivers' Handbook and should NOT be used with other books
(except for *I Can Make You Like Me* by Paul McKenna).

The *Top Gear Drivers' Handbook* is given away to all members of the
Top Gear Motoringists' Association. Non-members can purchase it from
many popular retail outlets, or simply pop into these retail outlets on your
lunchbreak and thumb through the book, idly looking at the short bits
of text and the pictures, as you are doing now, you cheapskate. This isn't
a library. Unless it is. In which case, sorry.

ABOUT THIS BOOK

Top Gear Drivers' Handbook is your guide to owning and operating a motor vehicle in the modern world. It aims to give simple, practical advice on a range of subjects including car buying, car maintenance and travelling abroad. Obviously, the crucial word there is "aims". James May "aims" to find the *Top Gear* studio without getting lost in Norwich, again. Richard Hammond "aims" not to go "Eeeugh!" every time he's presented with food from abroad. Jeremy Clarkson "aims" not to set everything he touches on fire. We all have aims and many of them are simply unachievable. This book is one of them.

Dear Fellow Motoringists,

Hullo, and welcome to the very latest edition of the *Top Gear Drivers' Handbook*, brought to you by the Top Gear Motoringists' Association. I sincerely hope that this book brings you a great deal of pleasure, whether you have bought a *Drivers' Handbook* for the first time or you have received this one as a replacement for last year's *Handbook* which, our lawyers have asked me to reiterate, MUST be returned to the TGMA immediately so that it can be completely destroyed before any more harm is done.

The Top Gear Drivers' Handbook aims to give simple, practical advice and guidance for anyone in charge of a motor vehicle. Set against the background noise of a modern world filled with telephones, popular music and people who like whistling, this book aims to be an oasis of calm and reason.

In many ways, this *Handbook* is very much like the TGMA Club itself, except that the book is almost certainly not located in Piccadilly, and even if it is, it would be relatively easy to move it towards

Mayfair, something that is almost impossible to do with the actual Club, as we found out to our considerable cost back in 1968. Furthermore, this book is made of modern lightweight materials such as paper and a slightly thicker sort of paper, whereas the TGMA Club is made of bricks and glass and various kinds of moss. I would like to reassure you that, unlike the TGMA Club, this book does not contain a foul-smelling back section that we really must get looked at.

So, to sum up, this book is like the TGMA Club itself except in most ways. Oh dear, I'm sorry Angela, this introduction isn't working at all. Read it back to me … actually don't bother, I'll come back to it later. I have to dash now, I've got to make this blasted presentation at my old school... actually, Angela, that reminds me, where did I go to school? And Angela, you can stop taking notes now, I've done with the intro … oh blast! Where's my other leg gone? Angela? For heaven's sake woman, put the bloody notepad down … ARRGH … my bloody REVOLVER'S GONE OFF AGAIN …

Sir Clark Sonhammond-Andmay
President, Top Gear Motoringists' Association

WELCOME TO
THE TGMA

THE HISTORY OF THE TOP GEAR
MOTORINGISTS' ASSOCIATION

The Top Gear Motoringists' Association was founded in 1871 by Sir Jeremiah Clarkson, Sir Rudyard Hammond and Lord May of Farting. At the time, "motoring" meant something quite different, which was why it came as some relief, not least to those living adjacent to the TGMA Club on London's Piccadilly when, 15 years later, the car was invented and the word "motoring" took on its familiar, more hygienic meaning.

Ironically, the late 19th century was a difficult time for the TGMA. Once its members discovered

Fig 1: Sir Jeremiah Clarkson, co-founder of the TGMA and inventor of the wildly exaggerated statement

Fig 2: Sir Rudyard Hammond, TGMA co-founder and host of the popular travelling circus "Totall Wypeout"

Fig 3: Lord May of Farting, third TGMA founder and explainer of torque (1872–1899)

that the meaning of "motoring" had changed, they lost interest and resigned from the club. The number of people who owned a motorcar was significantly lower than the number of people who were interested in that other thing, and the TGMA unwittingly found itself a sparsely populated organisation.

Happily, as car ownership began to climb so did TGMA membership and the organisation set out its guiding principles, many of which remain today. These include vows to give advice and guidance on motoring matters; to assist any member whose motor vehicle has failed to proceed; and to do everything within our power to help a member to cover up the mysterious death of their house-keeper. This last pledge was withdrawn in 1980, but the other principles remain to this day.

The TGMA has endured through the most turbulent times and though there have been some dark and regretful periods in its past, such as failing to revoke the membership of a Mr A Hitler until the summer of 1944, generally the organi-sation has kept its head held high and its stolen artworks well hidden.

Today, the TGMA boasts a membership of many thousands and can proudly claim to be the organisation to which any motorist can turn in times of need. Although just to reiterate, you are very much on your own with the whole murder thing.

> The TGMA – You can't see us,
> but we're behind you.

KEY DATES IN TGMA HISTORY

1871 - TGMA founded.

1914 - War.

1918 - Not war.

1939 - More war.

1945 - Less war.

1978 - Book of Top Gear Motoringists' Assocation history permanently misplaced.

You can contact the TGMA
by the following means:

Telephone: **London 5393 (ask for Neil)**

Telex: **443**

Fax: **London 72 (clearly mark
your fax "NOT for the
Petersen Clinic")**

Electronic mail: **generalenquiriesbythe
electronicmailsystem@
thetopgearmotoringists
apostropheassociation.com**

Postally: **The Top Gear Motoringists'
Association, Top Flat, 904A
Piccadilly, London, W1J 9HZ**

NOTE: Please do NOT telephone the number erroneously printed in
last year's *Top Gear Drivers' Handbook*. The Brazilian gentlemen who
answers is starting to sound extremely angry.

LEVELS OF TOP GEAR MOTORINGISTS' ASSOCIATION MEMBERSHIP

The Top Gear Motoringists' Association offers five distinct levels of membership, as detailed below. Prices are upon application.

Beige

Basic breakdown cover. Discounted travel insurance. Free picture of Liam Neeson. TGMA patrolman will adopt tissue-thin veneer of politeness concealing deep, deep well of hatred.

Blue

Enhanced breakdown cover including "Get you there" pledge. Admiring remark about your car. Five tons of topsoil, whether you want it or not. TGMA patrolman will address you as "Mister" followed by your surname (or a word that contains many of the same letters).

Sort of off-white, with a red border

Premium breakdown cover including "Take you somewhere nicer than the place you were planning on going to" pledge. Won't mention your speech impediment. A small pouch containing a plastic item of unspecified use. TGMA patrolman will address you as "Sir" until you feel important and then keep doing it until it's actually slightly embarrassing.

Plutonium

Gold cover giving assistance in the event of breakdown to every vehicle, appliance and person in your household. Also, pets. A really, really nice pen. TGMA patrolman will adopt a reverential but excessively chummy tone that may eventually slip into a faint but uncomfortable flirtatiousness.

Litotes

Mysteries solved, diseases cured, kitchen scissors found. Trained monkey. TGMA patrolman will treat you as a minor deity and make it absolutely clear that he is fully prepared to do absolutely anything for you, no questions asked.

ON THE ROAD

LAWS AND REGULATIONS

As an independent motoring organisation, the TGMA puts drivers' interests first. That is why we have a stout history of highlighting and questioning any rule of the road that we find absurd.

In 1973, for example, our then-president, Sir Cranleigh Elders-Churchmeadow, decided that the British tradition of driving on the left was outmoded and vowed to highlight his feelings by completing every journey on the right-hand side of the road.

Following Sir Cranleigh's arrest and imprisonment, his successor, Sir Hagley Warmingham-Chives, overturned this policy but introduced his own course of direct action against speed limits by driving everywhere at 100mph. In early 1974, with Sir Hagley sadly detained at Her Majesty's pleasure, he was replaced by Sir Charlton Merrychild-Grebe, a redoubtable former high court judge who took a more reasoned view of the law, with the exception of those statutes relating to the use of opium.

Following his arrest and imprisonment some two months later, the TGMA, under the guidance of new president Sir Marksby Denise-Richards, decided to set out a basic policy of law abidance, lest its members become confused by the previous 18 months' of conflicting, illegal and ultimately rather deranged advice.

To this end, the Top Gear Motoringists' Association now firmly states that the rules of the road are to be obeyed. Whilst we may object to, for example, the imposition of one-way streets in our cities (not least the street behind the TGMA Club in London), we must also remind members that to ignore such restrictions is highly inadvisable, especially if you are caught after a hearty lunch at the club and tell the attending police officer to "Sod the sodding hell off, you sodder." We are, of course, very much looking forward to seeing you again, Sir Christopher, just as soon as you are released.

We also generally advise against the use of opium and remind you that its consumption is forbidden inside any room at the TGMA Club, with the exception of the library.

There are other publications that deal with the rules of the road in more detail, such as the Ministry of Top Gear's *Alternative Highway Code*, but suffice to say the TGMA's official position is that one should take heed of these rules unless they are proving to be a bloody inconvenience.

As former TGMA president Sir Quillington Bray-sed-Lamb famously said shortly before he was sentenced, "Whatever one does or does not, the important thing is not to get caught."

MOTORINGISTS' ETIQUETTE

In its early years, the Top Gear Motoringists' Association was a stout exponent of basic manners on the road and this principle has endured ever since, barring a short hiatus during 1968 when the incumbent TGMA president became obsessed with bare-knuckle fighting and hallucinogens.

The Association laid down its bedrock of politeness in the early 20th century, when our patrolmen were instructed to salute any passing motorist whose vehicle carried a Top Gear Motoringists' Association badge. To this day, a TGMA patrolman will always acknowledge your car, be it with a salute (Gold membership and above) or a rude gesture and the throwing of a rock or small bag of dog waste (Mauve membership and below).

In the spirit of basic courtesy, the TGMA encourages members encountering each other out on the road to give a cheery wave. In doing so, each and every

TGMA member is drawn into a sacred bond of trust which may come in useful if we ever need to assemble a massed army of the night at short notice.

Fig 1: Gold membership and above.

Fig 2: Mauve membership and below.

Conversely, the TGMA does not endorse the modern habit of waving at those driving an identical car. It is our view that this is a strange and irritating practice with no earthly reasoning behind it. Yes, you have encountered another MGB or Triumph TR6. Almost anyone with the requisite amount of money could purchase such a thing and the ownership of this machine is not tantamount to joining some elite club or receiving a Nobel Peace Prize. If everyone engaged in such foolish behaviour we believe that newsagents would be full of people high-fiving and other such ghastly behaviour, simply because they shared the mutual appreciation of a given newspaper or chocolate bar.

Of course, the Top Gear Motoringists' Association cannot wholly condemn such pleasantries since they are infinitely preferable to the converse situation that may face the modern motorist. We refer, of course, to naked aggression and raw, ugly violence. The TGMA has always taken a dim view of such behaviour. Indeed, it has been one of our stated goals to stamp it out, particularly following the incident in 1980 in which beloved former TGMA President, Sir Wilson Morten-Harket, was called a "bell end" while at the wheel of his Armstrong Siddeley.

Fig 1: The unseemly practice of waving at a fellow motorist simply because they have the same car as you (even if it is a brown Morris Marina), should be avoided at all cost.

However, it would be naïve to suggest that tempers
cannot fray whilst at the wheel of a motoring vehicle.
It is all too easy to find that an otherwise pleasant
journey to meet an old friend for a hearty lunch
has suddenly turned into a horrendous knife attack
and subsequent high-speed chase from the scene.
So, in an attempt to make highway-based fracas less
dangerous and offensive, the Top Gear Motoringists'
Association has come up with a list of alternative
phrases that its members may deploy against another
motorist who has incurred their displeasure. Please
note these down and use them sparingly.

Fig 1: With firmness yet courtesy, a TGMA member deploys an
approved indication of displeasure from behind the wheel.

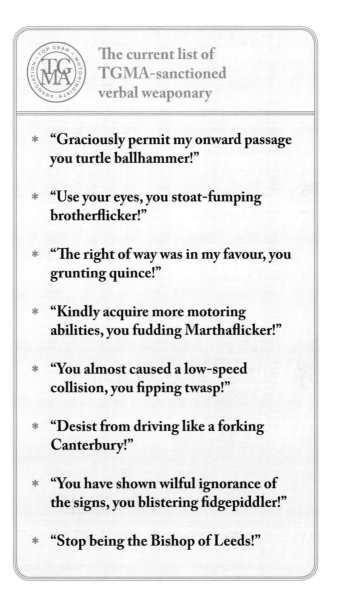

The current list of TGMA-sanctioned verbal weaponary

* "Graciously permit my onward passage you turtle ballhammer!"

* "Use your eyes, you stoat-fumping brotherflicker!"

* "The right of way was in my favour, you grunting quince!"

* "Kindly acquire more motoring abilities, you fudding Marthaflicker!"

* "You almost caused a low-speed collision, you fipping twasp!"

* "Desist from driving like a forking Canterbury!"

* "You have shown wilful ignorance of the signs, you blistering fidgepiddler!"

* "Stop being the Bishop of Leeds!"

GET TO KNOW YOUR CAR, INTIMATELY

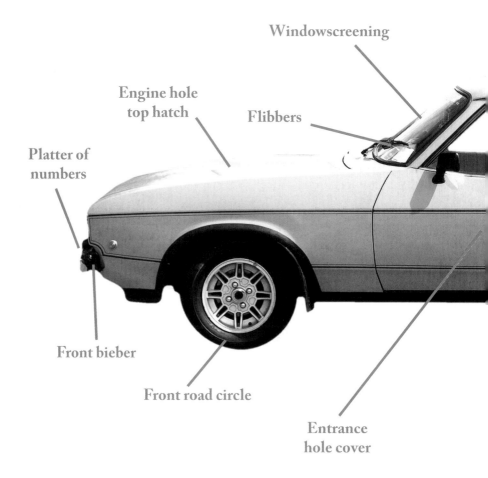

Windowscreening

Engine hole top hatch

Flibbers

Platter of numbers

Front bieber

Front road circle

Entrance hole cover

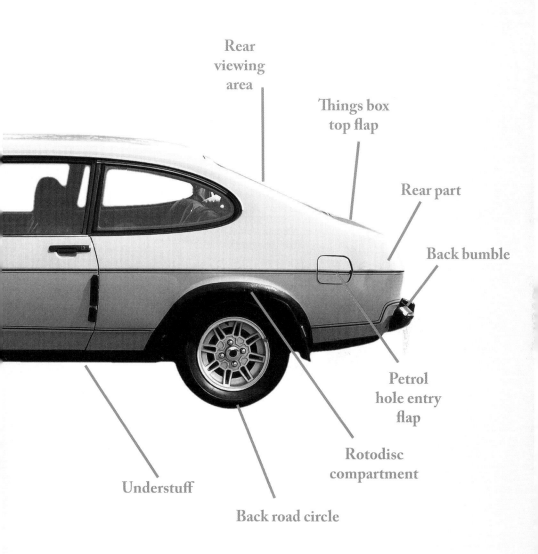

Rear
viewing
area

Things box
top flap

Rear part

Back bumble

Petrol
hole entry
flap

Rotodisc
compartment

Understuff

Back road circle

WHAT TO DO IN THE EVENT OF BREAKDOWN

As soon as you detect the first signs of a problem, pull in to the side of the road. This early sign can take many forms such as a small but unfamiliar noise, a large but unfamiliar ball of flame, or a sudden lack of forward motion caused by the presence of a wall or tree. In the latter case, please see the section entitled "How to decide if you have hit a wall or tree".

Once you have stopped, get out of the car. Contrary to the advice offered by some other organisations, do not put on a high-visibility jacket or vest, as these items actually make it easier for other motorists to hit you. The correct course of action is to make yourself as difficult as possible to see, perhaps by using dark clothing and a black balaclava. After all, how often do you see member of the SAS getting run over? Exactly.

Once you are out of the car, lift the bonnet and spend some time looking intently at the engine. It is a little-known fact that in absolutely no cases will the faulty component light up red and start shouting, "It's me! Here! I'm the bit that's broken!"

Fig 1: NO! This chap has made himself a highly visible target.

Fig 2: YES! This smart fellow will be very hard to hit.

Call the TGMA on the number provided, unless you are a Strontrium member or above, in which case project the agreed symbol onto the moon, as detailed during your induction weekend. Your TGMA patrolman will arrive shortly and punch you in the face (Brown membership and below) or attempt to fix your car (Palladium membership and above). If he is unable to repair your vehicle he will punch you in the face again (Gravel membership and below), transport you to the nearest garage (Chrysanthemum membership and above), or allow you to take his van and live in his house for as long as you deem necessary (Obsidian membership only).

While the TGMA patrolman is attempting to fix your car, it is advisable that you keep a safe distance away. Do not stand next to him fiddling with all his spanners and shouting "Oi! Cyril!" unless requested to do so.

If you wish to assist the TGMA patrolman, you could always get him a cup of tea. If your car does not have a kitchen, you should make arrangements to find one. Milk, one sugar, thanks.

In general, the causes of breakdowns can be split into three categories. There are simple problems, such as a faulty battery or cracked distributor cap; complex problems such as a blown head gasket or the Middle East peace process; and philosophical

Fig 1: There is no need for this sort of behaviour. After all, only 78 per cent of our patrolmen are actually called Cyril (or similar).

problems such as, "What is the point of your car?" With the exception of the blown head gasket, these problems can often be solved with a hammer and some WD-40.

In all likelihood, soon you will be on your way! If it proves impossible to restart your car, the patrolman will make arrangements to get you to your destination (Espiritu membership and above) or simply leave you wherever he found you until you are hunted down and eaten by wolves (Turdus membership and below).

WHAT TO DO IN THE EVENT OF BREAKDANCE

Try spinning on your head.

Fig 1: How to deal with the arrival of a breakdancing contest. See also "What to do if some Northern Soul gets jammed in the exhaust".

Items you should have in your car

It is highly advisable to make sure you have the following items in your car at all times, especially in bad weather:

* **A torch (battery-farmed).**
* **A flask of hot blankets.**
* **A warm tartan soup.**
* **A box of first aid.**
* **A toad-rope.**
* **Local hotels.**

Items your should NOT have in your car

It would be a tremendously bad idea to have the following items in your car at any time:

* **A torch (flaming).**
* **Loose soup.**
* **Lemurs.**
* **Fog.**
* **Another car.**
* **Despair.**

WHAT TO DO IF YOU GET A PUNCTURE

A puncture is caused by the air that should be in your tyre no longer being in your tyre and being somewhere else instead, e.g. the outside.

If your vehicle suffers a puncture, you have two choices. You can call the TGMA and request that a patrolman is sent out to change the punctured tyre for the spare (Red Panther membership and above), or you can get on and change the wheel yourself, you idle scum (Mauve Stoat membership and below).

If you are unsure as to whether you have a puncture or not, try to assess details such as:
- Rubbery burning smell.
- Sudden and catastrophic loss of control.

Alternatively, use the handy chart opposite.

Fig 1: This is a puncture.

Fig 2: This is not a puncture.

Fig 3: The puncture may be the least of your problems.

HOW TO CHANGE A WHEEL

One of the most common errors made when changing a wheel is to become confused and accidentally make a Victoria sponge. Here is the correct procedure for changing a wheel.

1. **Heat 8oz of butter in a pan and then mix it together with 8oz of caster sugar.**
2. **Beat 4 large eggs into the mixture.**
3. **Fold in 8oz of self-raising flour.**

4. **Line two cake tins with greaseproof paper and pour the mixture evenly into each tin.**

5. Place in an oven, pre-heated to 180°C (350°F/Gas mark 4) and bake for 20 mins.

6. After 20 mins, remove the tins and leave to cool. Remove from the tins, spread evenly with cream and strawberry jam and sandwich the two halves together.

7. Dust with icing sugar.

HOW TO MAKE A VICTORIA SPONGE

One of the most common errors when making a Victoria sponge cake is to accidentally change the wheel on your car. Here is the correct procedure.

1. Loosen the wheel nuts using the wheelbrace.

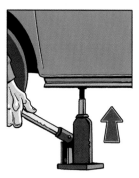

2. Jack up the car at the correct jacking point.

3. **Remove the wheel from the wheel hub.**

4. **Fit the spare wheel and finger tighten the wheel nuts.**

5. **Lower the jack and fully tighten the wheel nuts.**

He's got a firm purchase

Have you?

Gentlemen's Professional Driving Gloves

allow you to maintain an unshakeable grasp on…

- Steering wheels • Gear levers • Throats

British Formula 3 Runner Up **Diggy "Slippery" Pomade** says, *"Look, she was dead when I arrived! Now stop bothering me about your silly advertisement and go away!"*

Gentlemen's Professional Driving Gloves
The choice of the casual criminal. And drivers!

TGMA
INSURANCE

The Top Gear Motoringists' Association is delighted to offer its members a range of car insurance policies at worryingly discounted rates.

TGMA Insurance Services understands that in the unfortunate event of an accident you may need help with repairing your car, laundering your undergarments and finding the parts of you that appear to have fallen off. We realise this and we will do our best to help, but we are rather short-staffed at the moment. Also, we don't like you very much.

If you upgrade to our Manganese Plus policy you will enjoy several extra benefits. Firstly, in the event that your car is stolen or written off, you will get full use of a courtesy car for at least one afternoon a week, if Graham isn't using it. We also guarantee that we will answer the phone to you, wherever possible. And remember, all of our call centres are in the UK! Which is a bit of an inconvenience, given that our head office is in India.

Finally, if you upgrade to our Potassium Extra policy we will actually insure your car and turn a blind eye to most types of arson.

Did you know we also insure the following:
Pets!* Small aeroplanes! Inadvisable dares! Military coups! Nudism! Hats!

TGMA Insurance Services is registered with the Financial Services Authority. Registered as a cake shop, admittedly, but registered nonetheless. Please, let's not get bogged down in the whys and wherefores of that sorry business again. **TGMA Insurance Services, PO Box 533, London, India.** Leave parcels with Mrs Willingham upstairs.

* Not geese. Or dogs.

WHAT TO DO IF YOU HAVE AN ACCIDENT

First of all, it is important to establish that you have definitely had an accident. The chart (*opposite*) may assist you in your assessment.

There are other ways to assess whether you have had an accident:

* Had you only just shouted "watch this!"?
* Had you recently said "I'm sure it'll be fine"?
* Can you hear someone saying words such as "arrrgh!" Or "owww!"?
* Is that person you?
* Were you just put in mind of the rest of your life to date?
* Did your car just stop unexpectedly?
* Did it also change shape?
* Is there a stranger nearby, saying, "That looks a bit nasty..."

1. You have hit a wall.

2. You have hit a tree.

3. Now this is quite unusual.

4. Oh dear, it's happenend again.

Fig: 1: The four most common types of accident.

If you can answer yes to one or more of these questions, it is very possible that you have had an accident.

What to do next

Once you have established without reasonable doubt that you have indeed had an accident, you should assess the levels of your own injuries and consider whether you need to telephone one of the following:

* An ambulance.
* An undertaker.
* Ann, your wife.

If your accident has involved someone else, your insurance company will expect you to take down the other party's details unless your insurance company is TGMA Insurance Services, in which case it would be enormously helpful if you simply ran away and did not involve any of the authorities.

TGMA
LEGAL SERVICE

From time to time we all get into motoring scrapes that require assistance from the legal profession. There are many companies out there vying to help you with your insistence that you were not driving at the time or that your attempts to run her over were entirely unrelated to the divorce. These other companies will claim they have many years of experience and many examples of cases won against the odds. TGMA Legal Service is not like that. These firms may have a vast team of legal experts, testimonials from hundreds of satisfied customers, and an ability to remain sober throughout the morning, but only TGMA Legal Service has the legal brain and illegal legs of Sir Christopher Carruthers.

Sir Christopher's name will be familiar to anyone who has spent time on either side of the legal fence and slightly less familiar to Her Majesty The Queen who, we have been asked to point out, did not bestow upon him the knighthood he purports to possess.

Yet despite his wilful ignorance of the honours system, Sir Christopher is a man of the highest legal standing and his position at TGMA Legal Service promises to deliver creative misinterpretations of the law with a uniquely personal touch.

Your TGMA Legal Service membership provides you with a guarantee that whenever you require legal help, Sir Christopher will be on hand. As long as you understand that he is quite busy already. Plus, he doesn't work Thursdays.

TGMA LEGAL SERVICE
Because Legal and Illegal Are Basically the Same Thing

TGMA Legal Service should not be mentioned to anyone outside the circle of trust. TGMA Legal Service is registered as a 1979 Ford Escort van for reasons that we can't go into again.

TGMA Legal Service, Basement Flat, 904A Piccadilly, London, W1J 9HZ. Make sure you were not followed.

A GUIDE TO MAJOR BRITISH MOTORWAYS

Route: **London to Yorkshire**

Characteristics: **Witty, expansive, doesn't suffer fools gladly. Tells a marvellous story about the Bishop of York.**

Route: **London to Southampton**

Characteristics: **Has a black head and neck with a brown body and a white underside. Can be vicious if approached incorrectly.**

Route: **London to South Wales**

Characteristics: **Trained at RADA, turns grey in**

winter, claims to have invented the horse.

Route: Birmingham to Exminster

Characteristics: Easy to learn, but impossible to master. Leaks a blue-ish fluid when startled. Every two years is dismantled and rebuilt slightly to the left.

Route: Rugby to Gretna

Characteristics: Impervious to water but must not come into contact with anything from Sweden. Cheeky smile.

Route: Edinburgh to Glasgow

Characteristics: Three-octave range, allergic to wool, spends summers at Lake Como. Simply will not do stairs.

Route: London to Cambridge

Characteristics: Lasted from 1899 to 1901 with a great number of casualties. Was renamed "Starburst" shortly afterwards. Leafy smell.

Route: Outside London to the same bit of outside London

Characteristics: Loosely based on *The Old Curiosity Shop* by Charles Dickens, features on stamps, came second to Pete Sampras in 1997.

Route: London to Birmingham

Characteristics: Low, smooth and strawberry-flavoured. Long-running spat with Alan Rickman.

Route: **Bromsgrove to Measham**

Characteristics: **Bass / keyboards / backing vocals, still tours under the name Duke Gravy Incident.**

Route: **Manchester to back where you started**

Characteristics: **You know that feeling when you're really tired but you can't get to sleep? The opposite of that.**

Route: **Liverpool to Yorkshire**

Characteristics: **Chef, restaurateur, writer, broadcaster, chef, skydiver, amateur bullfighter and chef. Also a kind of stain that ruins aluminium.**

AARDVARK	AMPERSAND	BAXTER	BELMING	BUMBAG	CRESS	DAVE	DIPSWICH	DIVVY	EASBY	EAST COVENTRY	FRIGBY	GREASY	HOMIES	HOOPLA!	HOSIERY	N. WHORES	OOOOH
234																	
573	358																
123	456*	789															
346	475	743	655														
67	58	743	268	123													
666	666	666	666	666	666*												
890	583	498	234	53	493*	666											
234	588	298	72	84	185*	666	511										
692	24	267	267	5	48*	666	2	1									
123	588	345*	387	52	18*	666	287	477	168								
274	32	89	399	27	167*	666	268	63	174	68							
753	4	4	4	611	26*	666	4	83	168	276	711						
257	84	786	296	311	87*	666	173	57	257	387	200	257					
198	257	678	43	478	523*	666	39	15	299	256	238	456	549				
174	853	239	378	145	375*	666	268	234	127	456	25	280	56	198			
473	245	167	534	26543	468*	666	174	3	65	72	361	468	567	166	623		
347	478	14	6	186	456*	666	398	549	145	478	310	576	173	83	199	358	
852	247	289	167	78	367*	666	467	468	28	260	174	52	31	35	3*	174	395
685	55	378	251	260	256*	666	287	312	368	95	433	123	98	48	49*	368	468
231	236	444	154	89	395*	666	174	93	8	286	523	387	593	689	52	194	72
23	574	396	156	48	123*	666	284	456	71	72	352	367	267	281	247	32	58
786	342	268	214	567	256*	666	398	231	358	198	84	356	83	159	291	791	999
549	266	811	543	200	359*	666	234	41	417	257	167	69	254	287	592	389	168
257	236	43	28	169	943*	666	83	257	234	476	765	22	73	378	639*	194	5
532	376	287	589	296	52*	666	145	67	376	198	168	549	145	84	212	9	82
45	61*	83	174	198	469*	666	32	267	47	711	394	287	156	366	12	264	1
75	145	221	387	395	29*	666	154	311	248	467	307	359	91	72	94	612	-174
427*	399*	83	123	351	278*	666	267	432	132	34	174	49	173	37	234	63	549
247	41	234	487	278	754*	666	256	369	287	72	417	376	358	174	943	306	361
541	692	357	53	352	72*	666	174	17	589	269	655	342	362	583	289	456	35
946	63	167	386	528	518*	666	789	168	48	845	278	167	200	387	467	23	256
468	174	52	358	173	39*	666	247	38	364	94	185*	375	468	389	122	548	167
68	478	13	95	456	56*	666	222	372	488	287	946	15	222	83	489	594	300
3*	365*	174*	123*	72*	145*	666*	278*	12*	234*	159*	489*	118*	257*	52*	48*	645*	362*

DRIVING DISTANCES

In the modern world it is often hard to keep abreast of how far away different parts of Coventry are at the moment. This chart should help.

* Indicates use of a ferry

NORTH COVENTRY

167	ROGERMOORE															
93	396	SOUTH COVENTRY														
271	145	257	SPRINGSTEEN													
160	173	234	167	ULUM BATOR												
834	358	287	514	52	WARMLY											
413	200	378	2	43	297	WASPS										
154	354	52	145	387	483	623	WEST COVENTRY									
139	257	257	482	189	651	544	84	YESMAN								
890	326	511	268	378*	63	154	267	467	YOWSER!							
234	389	174	478	174	568	367	145	865	257	ZANCHESTER						
145	254	822	234	19	91	173	222	287	15	145	ZEDINBURGH					
52	85	198	549	287	287	456	48	284	655	478	95	ZEWCASTLE				
468	351	48	399	58	259	133	468	174	411	167	145	456	ZIRMINGHAM			
59	923	816	168	567	145	268	39	87	257	812	92	695	48	ZLASGOW		
234	509	351	26	65	36	165	451	174	43	173	482	456	76	268	ZONDON	
276*	222*	287*	267*	52*	15*	41*	598*	196*	36*	366*	256*	168*	257*	123*	1*	ZRISTOL

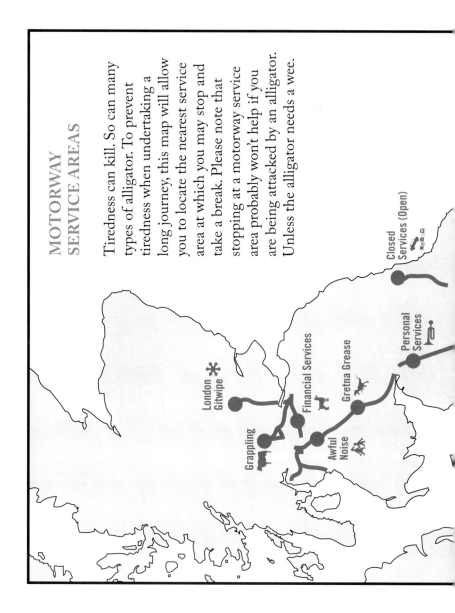

MOTORWAY SERVICE AREAS

Tiredness can kill. So can many types of alligator. To prevent tiredness when undertaking a long journey, this map will allow you to locate the nearest service area at which you may stop and take a break. Please note that stopping at a motorway service area probably won't help if you are being attacked by an alligator. Unless the alligator needs a wee.

Closed Services (Open)

Personal Services

Financial Services

London Gitwipe

Gretna Grease

Grappling

Awful Noise

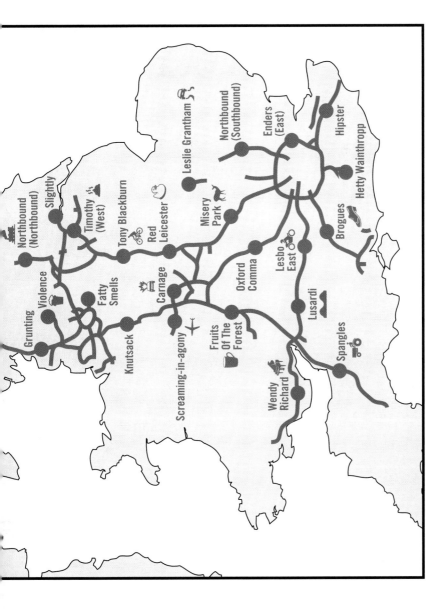

TOURING BRITAIN

ADVICE FOR MOTOR TOURISTS

Great Britain is a wonderful place in which to enjoy a holiday. As former Top Gear Motoringists' Assocation president Sir Clifton Undercroft-Sieves himself said back in 1974, "To holiday in Britain is to avoid having to talk to Johnny Foreigner, and that's a good thing." He was imprisoned soon afterwards for a very slightly related crime.

The benefits of taking a holiday in Britain are many and varied: easy access to a cup of tea; no requirement to speak an unfamiliar language; and, to quote Sir Clifton once again, "When it turns out to be bloody awful you can just go back home."

THE TGMA BACKS BRITAIN

The TGMA has always promoted British holidays and backed up this conviction with some simple, common-sense recommendations for places to stay and attractions to visit. This year these lists have been comprehensively updated to reflect feedback from our members, many of whom suggested that most of the hotels we were recommending were past their best, and that at least one of the walking routes needed some rather urgent amendment. It is the TGMA's hope that the brand new information contained in the following pages will no longer force you to sleep in a so-called "crack den" unless you absolutely want to. We are also confident that we will now lose fewer members to landmines, cliff erosion or an awful, awful ostrich incident.

REGION: SURREY

The Olde Ghillie's Leg

Lachgalasheildie, Peebleshire

Visitors to this charming Scottish inn are often struck by its low ceilings. Fortunately, there is a hospital less than 45 minutes away. The full Scottish breakfast is a must, especially when one remembers that the hospital is less than 45 minutes away.

REGION: SURREY

STUART HALL

Stillandsparklingwater, Cumbria

A charming country house of mid- to low-Victorian origin. Excessively furnished rooms offer a welcome place to hide away from the owners, who are ghastly.

REGION: SURREY

Hotel Y Ffronts

Llyllgllyllyllyllw, Gwynedd

Hidden away under an enormous pile of rocks, this guesthouse offers a deeply personal experience making it perfect for those seeking to make a clean getaway. If you like lamb you won't be disappointed, because there is one in every room.

REGION: SURREY

THE SITUATION

Llanhammer, Brecon Beacons, Powys

Difficult to find and even harder to leave, this eight-room hotel has been built in what was a rectory and, indeed, still is, much to the irritation of the local vicar. Food is not available anywhere.

REGION: SURREY

The Windshear Hotel

Jimdale, North Yorkshire

Delightful former school and slaughterhouse converted into an immodest hotel set amongst violently rolling countryside. Perfect for an abrasive walk followed by a pint of locally brewed Malty Cock real ale in front of a roaring fire engine.

REGION: SURREY

The Lingering Smell

Lower Sixthform, Derbyshire

The perfect spot from which to avoid the rest of the Peak District. Every room is furnished in a style, or at least claims to be. Restaurant boasts a range of freshly caught vegetables and a comprehensive water list.

REGION: SURREY

The Horsemeat Hotel

Stout-under-Garments, Gloucestershire

A rambling and incoherent old house set in 12 acres of other buildings, deep in the heart of Gloucestershire. Seven beautifully appointed rooms and seventeen badly decorated ones, plus an inadequately finished dining room.

REGION: SURREY

THE FLYE

BONO, NEAR THE EDGE, SHROPSHIRE

A delightful mid- to late-22nd century hotel, distinguished by its entirely silver exterior and ability to hover silently above the surrounding Shropshire countryside. Be aware that you might be harvested for organs.

REGION: SURREY

Creamy Cream Hotel & Creamery

Clotted Cream, Devon

A very rich and filling country hotel, so thick and creamy that you might find it extremely difficult to stand up. Or breathe. Staying longer than a couple of days can lead to pains in the left arm and a tightening of the chest.

REGION: SURREY

The Flatulent Labrador

Damon Hill, East Sussex

If you've always dreamt of finding a real life recreation of the 1980s situation comedy *'Allo 'Allo* tucked deep in the rolling Sussex countryside, this place will disappoint you. It's nothing like that at all. Strange smell.

REGION: SURREY

Olde Blacke Bearde's Retreate

Arrrrrrr, Cornwall

An unusual inn that aims to replicate the experience of being on a pirate ship, thanks to constantly moving floors, entirely incomprehensible staff and random bursts of cannon fire. Every guest receives complementary scurvy. Described by many as "simply too pirate-y".

REGION: SURREY

THE SODDING INN
Sodding, West Sussex

The main inn nestles deep within the heart of West Sussex, whilst the guest rooms are located in cottages deep within the lungs, large intestine, gall bladder and testes of West Sussex. The restaurant, meanwhile, is in an outbuilding, deep within the buttock crevice of West Sussex. Best avoided.

REGION: SURREY

The Cleavesden Golf Hotel
Saxophonist St Jonathan, Suffolk

Old pictures depicting classic golfing moments line the walls of this luxurious country hotel with its famous 19th Hole bar and acclaimed Nick Faldo Restaurant, all of which makes this the perfect retreat for anyone who loves golf. Particularly suitable for those who love golf but can't play it, since the hotel does not have a golf course.

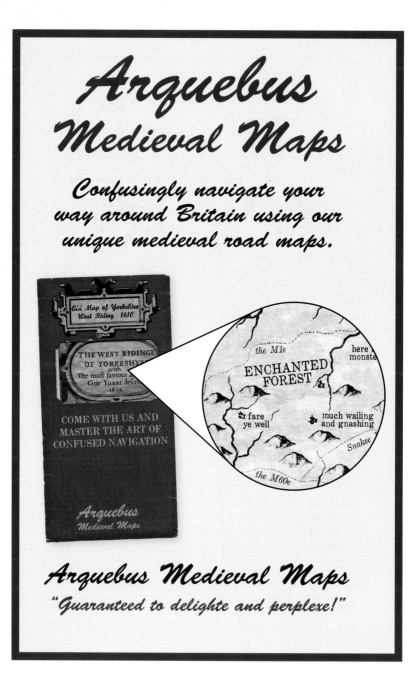

REGION: SURREY

THE ANTHRAX INN

Bramleyframlinghamham, Norfolk

Re-opened in 1998 following an unnecessarily long refurbishment, this quaint former coaching inn is entirely decorated in the style of popular American rock band Anthrax. Owner David Metaaaaaal admits the name has been problematic. "We've had literally no guests in over 12 years!" he quips, while weeping.

REMEMBER: Top Gear Motoringists' Association members receive a discount at the hotels listed. Simply give the receptionist the approved TGMA code upon checking in.

NOTE: It has been brought to our attention that the discount code given in last year's *Driver's Handbook* was causing problems at some hotels. As a result of this, from July 2011 the code will cease to be: "*I wish to kiss you*". Please make a note of the new code: "*There is a bomb in my bag*".

RECOMMENDED BRITISH TOURIST ATTRACTIONS

SCOTTISHLAND
The Rock of Glashieglochieglie
Glashieglochieglie, Farth

The biggest rock in the area, being about the size of a big table. The excellent visitors' centre at the base of the rock ironically rather dwarfs it and makes the rock impossible to see from most angles.

CUMBRIALAND
Wellingsmere Coughing Museum
Wellingsmere, nr. Helicopter
Recently revarnished, this wonderful museum offers a delightful history of the cough, stretching back to the invention of coughing in 1877. A wide range of coughs is on display and visitors can pick up their own cough in the gift shop on the way out. Café best avoided.

NORTHERNUMBRIA

Boots

Huxtable, nr. Cosby

For many years motorists on the B5432 near the remote village of Huxtable have found themselves saying, "What an unexpected place to find a branch of Boots!" Well worth a visit, especially if you are running low on deodorant, toothpaste or rubber gloves.

WESTERCHESTERER

Framlington Mouse Hospital

Framlington, Muesli

If you've ever wanted a closer insight into the sterling work done by mouse doctors, mouse nurses, mouse physiotherapists, mouse receptionists, mouse cleaners and mouse administrative staff, this is the place for you. Recently reopened after the awful events of 2010 when one of the staff turned out to be a cat in disguise.

SOUTH NORTHAMPSHIRE

Hollingsby Moaen

Upper Hollingsby, nr. Lower Hollingsby

According to the Domesday Book, a moaen was
a type of flat, flavourless bread used as a hat during
the famous moth attacks of 1052. Quite why this
word should also be used on a sort of ugly, stumpy
tower that is definitely not made of bread is
something no one really knows or cares about.
The former home of the actor Peter Bowles,
when he could be bothered.

CRESSCHESTER

The Forest of Trees

Wisdom, nr. Grimsdale

In 1872, wealthy local industrialist Deniston Welt announced what he believed to be an unprecedented plan to create a forest of trees. His employees were too scared to tell him that Britain already had many forests, all made of trees, and Welt's forest of trees was finished just days before he found out, at which point he became so furious that he sacked everyone and then invented the hand grenade.

BOOTSY COLLINS
Hemsby Castle
Hemsby, nr. Bemsby

A startling 15th-century building packed with so many fascinating facts that they will actually push existing information out of your head. As a result you may find yourself incapable of driving home again afterwards. There is a really angry robin in the gift shop that no one can do anything about. It's really angry.

HIGH WHISTLING
The Fax Machine Museum
Ofsted, nr. Ailing

A bad idea rendered utterly dreadful since it has been curated by a blithering idiot who knows nothing about fax machines. Contains several very basic errors, including the repeated assertion that fax machines use "magic", and a baffling section about turtles inexplicably entitled, "the aqua fax".

PYWYSYW
The Awkward Silence
Llanllanllanllanllan, nr. Snwcer

In this tranquil part of Wales lies a remarkable hillside known locally as The Awkward Silence. Visitors say that one minute they are enjoying the peace and quiet, the next they are uncomfortably shuffling their feet and becoming filled with an urge to clear their throats and say idle things about the weather.

WEST EASTLEY

Mnnnnnington House

Braply, Knees

The pointlessly annoying home of the Duke of Westerchester. Highlights include the "Chamber of Fact", in which one may learn that Polo mints are made in York; and the "Bee-o-drome", which is basically just a stupid room full of bees. Don't go into the gift shop. It's a trap.

NOTE: Showing your TGMA membership socks at any of the British tourist attractions recommended in this section will result in a 25 per cent increase in the entry fee and the possible attentions of the local constabulary, so please don't.

TOURING ABROAD

ADVICE FOR TOURING ABROAD

In this day and age, the TGMA is aware that some people prefer to holiday overseas rather than in Britain. To reflect this, the *Top Gear Drivers' Handbook* will henceforth refer to such places using the modern term "abroad" rather than, as in previous editions, the phrase "not Britain".

Holidaying "abroad" has many advantages. One can see fascinating new places, sample delightful new cuisines and experience levels of robbery and food poisoning simply not attainable at home. However, taking your car "abroad" is not for the faint-hearted, and you should first read these simple guidelines.

HOW TO
DRIVE ABROAD

Driving "abroad" is broadly the same as driving in the United Kingdom, but there are some key differences. First of all, it is worth remembering that most of the countries in Europe drive on the opposite side of the road, and one must adapt accordingly. It is generally considered bad manners to continue blithely driving on the British side of the road (traditionally known as the "correct" side) and to expect the motorists of your host nation simply to swerve out of your way. It is also quite dangerous, especially on an autobahn.

There are, of course, some countries that DO drive on the British (or "correct") side of the road. These include:

* Australia.
* Welsh Canada.
* India.
* Japan.
* Sweden (before 1967).
* Scotland.

Please note that in earlier editions of this book, the preceding list erroneously contained the word "France". The TGMA now accepts that this was a mistake and sincerely hopes not too many people were injured.

As a show of courtesy, whenever one is driving abroad one should attempt to blend in with the driving styles and standards of the country in which one is travelling. This can be achieved in the following ways:

* Hooting at girls.
* Parking wherever you feel like it.
* Swerving about like a bloody idiot.

Fig 1: The vehicular sexism gambit.

Finally, one should remember that most countries "abroad" use kilometres per hour rather than miles per hour, and one should not attempt to drive at 130mph on a motorway unless one wishes to suffer the same fate as former TGMA president, Sir Derek Leominster-Coombes, who will not see the outside of a French prison for another two to three years.

APOLOGY: An earlier edition of the *Top Gear Drivers' Handbook* may have given the erroneous impression that there is no such place as "Italy". We now accept that this is probably wrong.

EUROPEAN ATTRACTIONS

COUNTRY: FRANCE

L'Académie de Blaireau

Coulis de Framboises, Poirot

A fascinating school devoted entirely to teaching badgers to replace guide dogs for the blind. Described by former president Jacques Chirac as "dangerous beyond reason", the school nonetheless perseveres with its baffling work under the slogan, *La tuberculose pour tous!* (Tuberculosis for all!).

COUNTRY: FRANCE

Musée de L'armée de L'air de Singe

Chapeau sur Pamplemousse, L'Oooo

A delightful museum dedicated to France's unique Monkey Air Force, which operated between 1961 and 1979 with almost no success and the loss of several baboons. The entire operation was disbanded when it was belatedly realised that most monkeys quickly tire of flying an aeroplane and start indiscriminately strafing the ground with machine-gun fire.

COUNTRY: BELGIUM

La Cathédrale de Chats

Pommes dans les Cheveux, D'Oink

Under the stewardship of Fr. Lionel Blaire, this beautiful old church claims to be the world's only place of worship for cats. It is completely deserted as a result. The attached museum is largely devoted to the one occasion in 1974 when a cat inadvertently wandered into the building during a service (but then left almost immediately because it was bored and didn't like the choice of hymns).

COUNTRY: THE NETHERHOLLANDS

The Windmill of Death

Wjees, Jopp!

Dare you brave the blades to enter the windmill of death? Actually, yes. The blades move rather slowly and, upon closer inspection, are made of foam rubber. In fact, the entire facility has been built on the assumption that the average visitor has recently consumed an enormous quantity of marijuana.

COUNTRY: DENMARK

Verden af Hylderne Peter Schmeichel

Syborg, Legolund

Since retiring from professional football, ruddy-faced former Manchester United goalkeeper

Peter Schmeichel has returned to his homeland to set up this fascinating museum of shelves, featuring many different types of shelf such as free-standing shelves and the sort of shelves that are screwed to the wall. Actually not fascinating at all.

COUNTRY: SWEDEN

The Restaurant of Wood

Hjoooolstrum, Saab

If you like wood, you'll love this entirely wooden restaurant serving classic wooden dishes including butternut sawdust, oak steak and cherrywood trifle. Not suitable for anyone who wears dentures or possesses a digestive system that cannot process large quantities of wood. Be warned, the kitchen is almost constantly on fire.

Planning a motoring holiday overseas?

 If you're catching the motorcar ferry from Dover this summer, why not make the start of your holiday panicky and unpleasant by spending the preceding night at the Welmington Hotel.
Located just that little bit too far away from Dover, the Welmington Hotel guarantees you an unrelaxing stay during which you will worry almost constantly about what time you need to get up in the morning.

Every stay at the Welmington includes:
- ♈ Disconcertingly vague directions.
- ♈ Local maps with no scale on them.
- ♈ Wildly conflicting information about the proximity of the sea.

THE WELMINGTON HOTEL
Just some miles north-ish of Dover

COUNTRY: AUSTRIA

Das Haus Des Amüsantes

Geschescheschur, Arnie

Das Haus Des Amüsantes (or "The House of Amusing Things") is run by comedian Rudi Schreiber, "The Funniest Man in Austria" and famed for his "My dog's got no nose. How does it smell? It is incapable of smelling. I told you, it has no nose" routine. A small but upsettingly laid out museum of things he finds amusing, including a tiny pencil, a report on hat theft and a strange drawing of the American singer, Lionel Richie.

COUNTRY: WEST GERMANY

Die Frisur Prüfeinrichtung

Kopfsburg, Saxophone

Famed as Germany's most stringent hairstyle-testing facility, visitors can watch as the latest hairstyles are tested in important hairstyle areas such as hat resistance, spaciousness, crash safety and, of course, flavour. Described by none other than German travel writer Klaus Gesperg as "really strange".

COUNTRY: SPAIN

El Museo de Batas Robadas

Esporta, Cacacaca

The Museum of Stolen Bathrobes was founded in 1978 when its founder, Fernando Estello, took a towelling dressing gown from the Best Western Calamares Tortillas hotel in Madrid. Since then his collection has grown to over three, all of which are displayed here. It's worth phoning ahead before your visit, as Estello runs the museum on his own and is frequently being arrested for other crimes.

COUNTRY: SPAIN

La Historia del Zumo de Naranja

Zestos, Sunnidee

If you thought the history of orange juice would be straightforward and rather boring, you would be right. It is. However, that hasn't stopped a local lunatic from setting up an unnecessarily enormous museum to chart its deeply tedious story. Attempting to leave early may result in you having a water pistol full of orange juice fired at your clothes and face.

NOTE: The Norwegian National Museum of Cheesing no longer features in this guide as it is closed again for the same reason as last time.

TGMA AFFILIATES IN EUROPE

The Top Gear Motoringists' Association has several affiliated breakdown organisations who may be able to assist you if your motor vehicle fails to proceed, or succeeds in proceeding at a time when it was rather unfortunately parked just in front of the sea. You may contact them as follows:

France
Assistance Malheureusement
+33 48-332 382 2822 0

West Germany
Kaputgerhelper
+49 8-366 034-4 9-2228 (422) 8

Spain
Las RAC
+34 53 3 5377 382 4 632 63-2 5532(7) 32-222 24

Scotland
All Right There Pal?
Peebles 6

CAR MAINTENANCE

THE IMPORTANCE OF
CAR MAINTENANCE

Owning a car is very much like owning a dog.
You must remember at all times to give it fuel and
to regularly exercise it, and you must ensure that
at strict intervals it receives the attentions of a
professional who can inform you of problems that
may have escaped your notice, such as a malfunc-
tioning wheel-bearing or a missing leg.

In between those scheduled visits to the garage (or,
in the case of the dog, to the vet and subsequently
the police station) it is vital that one performs a
series of basic checks.

In the dog's case, simply pat its head and see if its tail wags. If it does, the dog is probably working correctly. There is no need to undertake more in-depth tests unless you wish to suffer the same fate as former TGMA president Sir Jackson Marks-and-Spencer, whose attempts to "take the dog's temperature" led to his swift imprisonment.

Fig 1: The simple way to check that your dog still works.

In some ways, the car is less complex than the dog. It can be left alone for several days and still function thereafter, something the average canine signally fails to do. Furthermore, if some part of the car accidentally becomes detached it is a relatively easy and mess-free process to reattach it, and something that can be observed by your young daughter without prompting her to scream almost constantly for the next three weeks.

For this reason, it is possible to open up parts of the car and perform basic adjustments to its workings. Contrary to advice given in editions of the *Top Gear Drivers' Handbook* published between 1921 and 1975, this is NOT something we would recommend you attempt with your dog.

In order to facilitate the basic maintenance of your car, it is important to familiarise yourself with the fundamental parts of the engine, as follows:

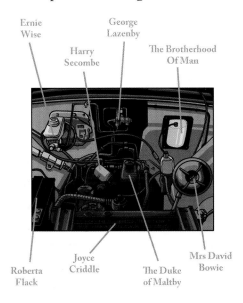

Ernie Wise

George Lazenby

Harry Secombe

The Brotherhood Of Man

Roberta Flack

Joyce Criddle

The Duke of Maltby

Mrs David Bowie

Fig 2: The full cast of Friday Night At The Ipswich Hippodrome.

BASIC MAINTENANCE

Here are some simple tasks you should attend to regularly:

* Fendistrate the grolling spring.
* Re-grist the front and rear mole wrists.
* De-obviant the Prestwick bulb.
* Cork off the lumsden plates (upper and side).
* Molliate all seven quist knees.
* Clean or replace the Gnisp Jesus.
* Dillient the roper sleeves.
* Undillient the roper sleeves.
* Hudder the Leicester bearings (x 2).
* Smoothiate the Orsp Kettle™.

TYRES

"Tyres are the windows to the hands of the heart of the motor vehicle." So said former TGMA president Sir Devon Bouvediere-Sloves, shortly before he was convicted for possession of over 12lbs of high-grade opium. Nonetheless, his wildly hallucinating point still stands today. Tyres are

Put a

Badger
in your car!

**Badger petrol is the only petrol
with bits of real badger in it***

You know it's Badger by the stripe!
And the appalling smell!

* Pending the results of a Ministry of Transport investigation

hugely important in areas such as acceleration, braking, cornering and not crashing. It is therefore of utmost importance that your vehicle's tyre pressures are kept in line with the manufacturer's recommendations.

Here are some popular tyre pressures:
* 32 psi
* 28 psi
* 2.2 bar
* 3.0 bar
* 120 ooms
* 0.12 y (US)
* Oh! (std 543 EU)
* 15,000,000,000,000,000,000 Clarksons

Here are some other pressures:
* Money.
* Health.
* The child.
* Oh God, she's found them.
* I think there's someone downstairs.
* That really has never happened before.
* Mostly my idea, yes.
* Honestly, I'm looking after it for Sir Devon Bouvediere-Sloves.

HOW TO REMOVE A MAN CALLED STEVEN FROM YOUR BOOT

Fig 1: Open the boot.

Fig 2: Ask Steven to get out of the boot.

Fig 3: Problem solved!

VISIBILITY

As first noted in the *Top Gear Drivers' Handbook 1977*, "I'm sorry officer, I simply didn't see it, or you, or it!" is no longer an admissible excuse for common driving errors such as ploughing into the side of a police horse, running over a police motorcyclist and then smashing through the front of a police station. That is why visibility should be of paramount concern for anyone who wishes to avoid such a fate and the subsequent imprison-ment / loss of TGMA presidency that it entails.

Items to put in your windscreen washer bottle
* Windscreen-washer fluid.
* Water.

Items NOT to put in your windscreen washer bottle
* Soup.
* Dust.
* Thoughts.
* Hope.

Maintenance Record

Use this handy page to keep a record of the basic maintenance tasks you have performed on your car.

☐ Check tyres   DATE ....

☐ Stains covered   DATE ....

☐ Check upholstery   DATE ....

☐ Damage concealed   DATE ....

☐ Check trousers   DATE ....

☐ Worst bits tapped out   DATE ....

☐ Czech embassy   DATE ....

☐ Numbers filed off   DATE ....

☐ Cheque bounced   DATE ....

☐ Full re-spray   DATE ....

CAR BUYING

PURCHASING A MOTORCAR

Buying a car can be a complicated and stressful business. In the early 1970s, the Top Gear Motoringists' Association attempted to address this unfortunate situation with its own, highly radical, used-car purchasing scheme. Unfortunately, it closed down in 1973 as it was too far ahead of its time. Also, too many people died.

Since then the TGMA has done what it can to help the car buyer by other, less frenetically rotating means. The following pages offer some simple, practical advice that will, for the most part, keep your arms and head attached to your body.

FINDING THE RIGHT CAR FOR YOUR NEEDS

When looking for your next motorcar, it is vital to consider what it is that you expect from it. If the answer is "Cleaner shoes", "Piping hot cakes" or "Toast, please!" then it is possible you have fundamentally misunderstood the meaning of the word "car" and indeed every aspect of this book so far. Assuming, however, that you are quite clear on what a car is and does, have you thought long and hard about what you will use it for? The needs of a busy executive, for example, are quite different from those of an escaped arsonist. Likewise, the requirements of an amateur pirate could be quite separate from those of a Norwegian goose-balloonist. That is why the TGMA has compiled the following questionnaire in order that you might reflect at some length and firmness on what you require from your next car.

How much space do you require?

☐ Lots ☐ Some ☐ None whatsoever

How many doors would you like?

☐ Two ☐ Four ☐ Seven ☐ Loads

Which of these is most important to you?

☐ Looks ☐ Personality ☐ Non-smoking

Which of these will you most use your car for?

☐ Business ☐ Pleasure ☐ Displeasure ☐ A clean getaway

Where will you keep the car?

☐ Garage ☐ Street ☐ Upstairs ☐ Leather pouch

Rank these attributes in order of importance

☐ Economy ☐ Height ☐ Flavour ☐ Looks like Janet

Which of these words best describes your personal
circumstances?

☐ Brittle ☐ Oily ☐ Untenable ☐ Just outside Leeds

Now complete this tiebreaker.

I need a new car because of what happened in or on…

....

....

....

....

....

PURCHASING A NEW CAR

Buying a new car can be a baffling experience, and one that often descends into petty haggling and raw, ugly violence. Time and again, surveys about the activities people least enjoy demonstrate that "Dealing with a car salesman" rates below "Home dentistry" and "Gutting another turtle of that size". Yet it does not have to be this way. If you are forearmed with some simple facts, you will enter the negotiations for your next car in a far stronger position.

Fig 1: A car salesman unleashes his vile arsenal of balloons.

Before you enter the showroom, remember these simple points:

* Car salesmen are mammals.
* Their vision is based on movement.
* They can run faster upstairs than down.
* They can move at speeds of up to 20kph (12mph) through water.
* They communicate by rubbing together very, very quickly.

From this information we can quickly see that car salesmen are extremely simple creatures. We see further evidence of this in the techniques they use to attract customers to their showrooms. These include:

* Opening all the hatchbacks.
* Brightly coloured signs.
* Helium balloons.

In other words, the car salesman assumes that you are six years old. Ergo, it should be relatively simple to outwit him. Unless you are, in fact, five.

PURCHASING A USED CAR

Used-car salesmen are a type of lizard and should be approached with caution. If possible, bring a sword.

When looking to buy a used car, pay very close attention to the vehicle you are considering. Always take the time to assess the following:

* Does the mileage tally with the amount of damage?

Fig 1: An accurate impression of a typical used car salesman.

* Was the model in question known for having a wet patch there?
* Should those numbers be written in Biro?
* Whose finger is it?
* Why is he attacking you with a piece of wood?

IS THE CAR YOU ARE THINKING OF BUYING ON FIRE?

It is a sad fact that some used-car salesmen may attempt to pass off a vehicle that is unfit for purpose. A recent survey by Trading Standards officers found that up to 86 per cent of second-hand cars were partially, or completely, on fire. With this in mind, watch out for the following signs:

* Smoke
* Flames
* Really quite hot

If you believe the car you were hoping to test drive is on fire, roll around on the ground for a bit and then walk away.

HOW TO SELL YOUR CAR

Selling your car privately is a good way to maximise the price you receive for it while avoiding the unwelcome attentions of those who might ask awkward questions such as, "What caused this dent?" and, "Didn't I see this on the news recently?"

In order to make selling your car as quick and unsuspicious as possible, you should take time to compose a short, but well-worded advertisement for it. Here is an example of how NOT to advertise your car:

VAUXHALL ASHTRAY

Don't know the year. It's about five, I think. Blue-ish. Smells *weird*. I mean, *really weird*. Sometimes does this vibrating thing. No seats. **£4,000**

This advertisement is badly worded and contains extraneous information that may arouse suspicion. Your advert should impart simple, comprehensive facts about age, mileage and equipment levels, as in this example:

FORD ESCORTE.
23,000 miles. Unusually red. Turbot diesel, 5-speed manly gearbox. Leather paint, metallic seats, hair conditioning, alloy windows, electric wheels, central looking, saturnine navigation. Very ecumenical, ideal family carp. **£39,990.**

RECALLS

The modern motorcar is an extremely sophisticated machine fitted with features we now take for granted, such as electrical windows, centralised locking and brakes that work. The downside of this complexity is that sometimes the brakes don't work and fail to stop the car before a branch of WH Smith does the job for them.

Naturally, car manufacturers monitor all potential faults and will issue a recall notice the instant they become aware of a design flaw that may compromise your ability to swerve around the flower stall if you choose to. There follows a list of recent recall actions applied to a range of popular models. If you find your car on this list you should immediately take it to the supplying dealer and march into the showroom screaming, "I could have been KILLED you idle SCUM!" until the kitchen-appliance salesman reminds you that the car dealer moved to new premises last year.

Model	Reason for recall
BMW X-Wife	Windscreen has raisins in it.
Citroen C-Section	Unacceptable views about Stoke-on-Trent.
Fiat Pustilion	Driver's seat smells of Nicholas Witchell.
Ford Fajita	Grumpy handbrake.
Honda Accordion	A lot of moths inside. A LOT.
Mercedes Art-Class	Handbook describes wrong kind of crisps.
Nissan Sputum	Do NOT look in the glovebox.
Renault Migraine	Wheels fitted upside-down.
Toyota Anius	May bring on goose allergy.
Volkswagen Rolf	Strange man in back seat.

FURTHER INFORMATION

FORTHCOMING TGMA EVENTS

The Top Gear Motoringists' Association is proud to sponsor various motoring-related and cultural proceedings through the year. Here are some of these forthcoming events.

The 47th Annual Harrumph

SATURDAY 25 JUNE

The Havers Arena, Chichester

A beloved fixture on the TGMA calendar in which retired colonels and purse-lipped ladies meet up to make disparaging noises about everything. Topics for the 47th Harrumph will include "Young peoples' clothes" and "That Welsh chap on the news, well you can hardly understand a bloody word he says!"

The Running of the Susans

FRIDAY 22 JULY

Chesney Hawkes, Gloucestershire

Cancelled in 2010 after the disgrace of the 2009 event, in which the winner was discovered to be called Jane, the Running of the Susans is back for 2011 and bigger than ever, with the promise that up to nine Susans will take part, terrorism permitting.

The Surrey Shit Dogs Show

SATURDAY 30 / SUNDAY 31 JULY

Tetanus Showground, Flatley

A delightful two-day celebration of feckless, inept and malodorous canines, featuring a live action arena hosting hourly displays of hopeless disobedience and rank inability to retrieve a stick. Features plenty of opportunities to get snarled at, bitten or covered in dog saliva.

Pointing at That Man

SATURDAY 13 AUGUST

Moirae Stuarte, Fyfe

For centuries people have travelled from miles around to spend the day pointing at a man in a field. This year's man is Steven Clepps of Grunting, who says he has been in training for eight months and can take any amount of pointing without falling over.

The James May Baroque Classics All-Nighter

SATURDAY 27 / SUNDAY 28 AUGUST

Pontins, Camber Sands, Sussex

The Top Gear Motoringists' Association's musical director will be spinning some phat 17th- to mid-18th century classics from dusk until dawn in this legendary functional tonality smackdown.

Please note: The TGMA operates a strict no-drugs policy at this event. Anyone caught with banned substances such as Sanatogen, Berocca or cod liver oil capsules will be asked to leave and may have their reading glasses confiscated.

The Lansbury Soup Flume

SATURDAY 3 / SUNDAY 4 SEPTEMBER

Hecksby Melba, Wilts

After the enormous success of last year's event, veteran actress Angela Lansbury will once again set up her extraordinary soup flume and invite passers by to have a go. The *Murder, She Wrote* star promises several improvements for 2011 including more flavours, less scalding and fewer sharp objects in the landing zone.

The Sudlingham Amateur Aerobatics Festival

SATURDAY 24 SEPTEMBER

Sudlingham, Woks

Described by one national newspaper as "harrowing and almost incomprehensibly dangerous", the Sudlingham Amateur Aerobatics Festival returns against all odds for a second year with the promise that if you can tell left from right and don't have any pressing need for your arms in future, you can have a go in one of their surprisingly flimsy stunt aircraft. Really not suitable for childen of any age or type.

The Hits of Fleetwood Mac Played On a Bassoon

FRIDAY 18 NOVEMBER

Flipping Blimey, Whisk

Following last year's acclaimed performance of U2's *Achtung Baby* album on a euphonium, local musician, raconteur and unconvicted sleeves thief, Mike Yesby, will embark on his most ambitious project to date, as he makes much loved songs including "Rhiannon", "Go Your Own Way" and "Dreams" almost completely impossible to enjoy.

NOTE: Keep an eye on local press for details of other TGMA events as they are announced. Unfortunately the Sunningsby Machine Gun Golf Contest won't return until after the inquest.

OTHER TGMA SERVICES

The Top Gear Motoringists' Association is rightly famed as a breakdown service, an insurance provider, and as the proprietor of a longstanding gentleman's club on Piccadilly, where retired high court judges can enjoy a warm and strange-smelling environment in which to make casually misogynist remarks. But there is much more to the TGMA than that. We are also:

* A loan shark.
* A fencing contractor.
* The government of a small West African country.
* A type of liquid.
* The missing answer to 12 across.
* The third single from Lady Gaga's first album.
* A weekend in Suffolk.
* Needlessly pessimistic.
* Totally unaware of the word "spherical".

The Top Gear Motoringists' Assocation
So much more than black-and-white
vans with a yellow flashing light on top
(although, in fairness, we are that as well).

OTHER PUBLICATIONS FROM THE TOP GEAR MOTORINGISTS' ASSOCIATION

THE TOP GEAR DRIVERS' HANDBOOK
Talking Book Edition

William Shatner reads out this book in a rather odd way. Not suitable for children.

THE TOP GEAR DRIVERS' HANDBOOK
Singing Book Edition

Mariah Carey sings this book accompanied by over 19 hours of original compositions. Contains at least 653 unnecessary notes. Not suitable for dogs.

THE TOP GEAR DRIVERS' HANDBOOK
Mime Edition

Insufferably lengthy reinterpretation of this book by Les Artistes Du Silence of La Rochelle. You cannot have your money back. No.

THE TOP GEAR DRIVERS' HANDBOOK TURNED INTO A CLOUD OF NON-TOXIC GAS

This entire book cleverly turned into a cloud of non-toxic gas for quick and easy inhalation. Ideal for the busy and the illiterate. Warning: We are not entirely sure that this works. Or that it is non-toxic.

FROM THE BAR TO BEHIND BARS

by Sir Bedwin Damon-Albarn

The remarkable memoirs of a former TGMA president, covering his life as a barrister and his incarceration for a moment of indiscretion that doesn't bear repeating when we all heard quite enough about it in the newspapers at the time.

THEY'LL GET YOU IN THE END

by Sir Wellsby Chipping-Campden

A light-hearted autobiography by another former TGMA president, now serving time at Her Majesty's pleasure for a series of thefts that his family have kindly asked us not to mention until the appeal is finalised.

SHE WAS LIKE THIS WHEN I GOT HERE

by Sir Egan McVities-Digestive

An often hilarious canter through the rich and varied life of the notorious former TGMA president, now enjoying his retirement inside HMP Parkhurst thanks to an incident we're sure everyone is aware of by now.

THE CASE FOR THE DEFENCE

by Sir Kebbesleigh Sheffield-Wednesday

The legendary former TGMA president mounts a spirited, highly personal and potentially libellous analysis of the evidence behind his conviction, rather glossing over the number of items that were found in his house and pockets.

TGMA Turbo Tunes!!!

The Top Gear Motoringists' Association is proud to announce a brand new cassette tape of music for your driving pleasure!

Each track has been lovingly re-recorded to incorporate a crass, car-based pun for no sodding reason whatsoever.

Featuring…

A-Ha – "The Sun Always Shines on TVR"
Nirvana – "Losing My Reliant"
The Charlatans – "The Only M1 I Know"
Madonna – "Ray of Citroen 15 Light"
Michael Jackson – "Rockin' Reliant Robin"
New Order – "Blue Mondeo"
Survivor – "Eye of the Sunbeam Tiger"
Rolling Stones – "Paint it Mercedes CLK Black"
The Smiths – "Girlfriend in a Commer"
Al Green – "Take Me to the Rover"
U2 – "Beautiful Daewoo"
Guns N' Roses – "Sweet Child o' Mini"
Bee Gees – "How Deep is Your Glovebox?"
Take That – "Relight My Pontiac Firebird"
Beach Boys – "Help Me Honda"
Lady Gaga – "Poker Fiats"
Phil Collins – "In the Fiat 500 Twinair Tonight"
Oasis – "Champagne Super Vauxhall Nova"
Billy Joel – "It's Still Rock and Rolls-Royce to Me"
The Eagles – "Hotel Ferrari California"
R.E.M. – "Shiny Happy People Carrier"

INDEX

TGMA APPLICATION FORM

TITLE ☐ Sir ☐ Dame ☐ Archbishop ☐ Generalissimo
☐ Mr ☐ Girl Mr ☐ Unmarried girl Mr

LAST NAME . . . .

FIRST NAME . . . .

MIDDLE NAME(S) . . . .

SIDE NAME(S) . . . .

GANG NAME(Z) . . . .

DATE OF BIRTH . . . .

HOUSE NAME . . . .

HOUSE NICKNAME . . . .

MOTHER'S MAIDEN VOYAGE . . . .

FLAVOUR . . . .

PREVIOUS CONVICTIONS . . . .

DID YOU PACK THESE BAGS YOURSELF? ☐ Yes ☐ Certainly not

PREFERENCE ☐ Orange juice ☐ Dust allergy ☐ Free pens

LEVEL OF TGMA MEMBERSHIP REQUIRED
☐ Platypus ☐ Yeasty ☐ Cress ☐ Soil ☐ Abusive

SIGNATURE TUNE . . . .

☐ From time to time the Top Gear Motoringists' Association may get into a
spot of bother with the taxman and will raise money by selling your personal
details to a range of disreputable organisations such as extortionists, fraudsters
and a man in China who keeps asking if you want to buy some magnesium. If
you DO want to NOT receive NONE of these offers then do NOT forget to
neglect to unTICK this box.

☐ I have pretended to read your terms and conditions.

☐ I am blissfully unaware of that time you left 2000 people's bank details in the
back of a minicab.